Contents

What is birth?

The birth of a child is an important event, and not just for the baby and his or her parents. The baby is born into a family group, a social group and also often into a religious community. All these groups have ways of marking this first rite of passage.

The ceremonies, rituals and celebrations with which a new baby is greeted vary from one religion to another, one country or society to another and even from one family to another. But most have a number of things in common, and express many of the same feelings.

Some rituals are protective, and may begin even before the baby is born. Pregnant mothers may ask for divine help to protect their unborn child and guide it safely into the world.

Once the baby has arrived, there are ways of offering thanks, through either prayer or ceremonies. There are also celebrations: parties, feasts and customs such as giving out sweets or 'wetting the baby's head'. Originally this phrase referred to the water sprinkled on a baby's head during baptism; now, especially in the United Kingdom, it also means enjoying a drink with friends and family to rejoice in the baby's birth and toast his or her health and future.

The birth of a child is a joyful rite of passage, marked by all religions.

This stained glass window shows a Christian image, in which the birth of Christ is celebrated by the three wise men. Each wise man carries a gift for the newborn baby: frankincense, myrrh and gold.

An important part of bringing the new baby into the family and community is giving the baby a name. Names have special importance. They give us our identity and are often chosen for their meaning or religious significance, or because they are associated with special people or qualities. Naming ceremonies are found in almost every religion and culture.

This book highlights birth traditions, ceremonies and customs in six major world religions: Christianity, Judaism, Islam, Hinduism, Buddhism and Sikhism. It also looks at practices in several other cultures.

FOCUS ON:
Gifts for the newborn

Bringing gifts to a newborn is one of the oldest traditions in human history. Many stories in religion and folklore describe the bringing of gifts to newborn babies, and the practice is more popular than ever today. In some places, gifts are given even before the baby is born – in the United States, for example, a pregnant woman's female friends and relatives throw a 'baby shower' for the mother-to-be, bringing presents of baby clothes, blankets, nappies and other things the new parents will need. In some cultures, gifts for the new baby have a protective function, such as religious medals and amulets. In most cultures, baby gifts are connected in some way with helping the child through life. In Western Europe and North America, money boxes, as well as cups, bowls and spoons – representing the food the child will need once he or she is weaned – are popular christening gifts.

Why are Christians baptized?

To become a Christian, a person must be baptized. Parents who want their children to be Christians welcome their babies with a baptism ceremony, in which the child is formally made a Christian and joins the Christian community. The baptism ceremony is carried out by a priest or minister.

John the Baptist, the cousin of Jesus, preached that people should be cleansed of their sins by bathing in the River Jordan. Jesus asked John to baptize him. Christians believe that as John was baptizing Jesus, he heard the voice of God saying, 'This is my beloved Son,' and he knew that Jesus was the Messiah. Christians today show that they accept Jesus as their saviour by following his example and being baptized.

Original sin was committed by Adam and Eve when they ate from an apple given to them by Satan.

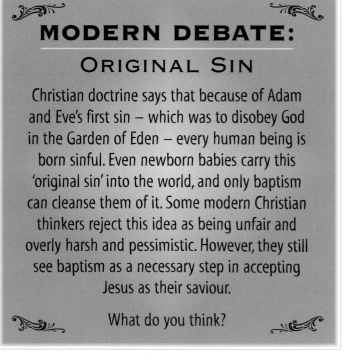

MODERN DEBATE:

ORIGINAL SIN

Christian doctrine says that because of Adam and Eve's first sin – which was to disobey God in the Garden of Eden – every human being is born sinful. Even newborn babies carry this 'original sin' into the world, and only baptism can cleanse them of it. Some modern Christian thinkers reject this idea as being unfair and overly harsh and pessimistic. However, they still see baptism as a necessary step in accepting Jesus as their saviour.

What do you think?

...Y OF LIFE

...rth

Randall

WAYLAND

12696651

First published in 2015 by Wayland
Copyright © Wayland 2015
All rights reserved.
1 3 5 7 9 10 8 6 4 2
Dewey number: 203.8'1
ISBN: 978 0 7502 9637 3

Produced for Wayland by Calcium
Design: Paul Myerscough and Emma DeBanks
Editor: Sarah Eason
Editor for Wayland: Katie Powell
Picture research: Maria Joannou
Consultant: Sue Happs

Wayland is an imprint of Hachette Children's Group
Part of Hodder & Stoughton
Carmelite House, 50 Victoria Embankment
London EC4Y 0DZ

Printed in China

Alamy Images p. 35 (ArkReligion.com), p. 39 (David Cherepuschak), p. 33 (Devinder Sangha), p. 29 (J. Marshall/Tribaleye Images), p. 22 (Jeremy Graham), p. 23 (mediacolor's), pp. 13, 15 (Nir Alon), p. 41 (Sue Bennett); **Circa Religion Photo Library** p. 32 (John Smith); **Corbis** p. 19 (Bazuki Muhammad/Reuters), pp. 26, 27 (Gideon Mendel), p. 37 (Kapoor Baldev/Sygma); **Dreamstime** pp. 12, 36, 43; **Getty Images** p. 24 (AFP Photo/Devendra M Singh); **Istockphoto** pp. 4, 5, 8, 17; **PA Photos** p. 25 (AP Photo/ Anupam Nath); **Panos Pictures** p. 20 (Warrick Page); **Photofusion** p. 30 (Judy Harrison); **Rex Features** p. 14 (A Snow/Israel Sun), p. 9 (Eye Ubiquitous); **Shutterstock** pp. 7, 11, 21, 31, 38, 42; **World Religions Photo Library** p. 18 (Christine Osborne).

Cover photograph: **Alamy Images** (Steven Lee)

An Hachette UK company
www.hachette.co.uk   www.hachettechildrens.co.uk

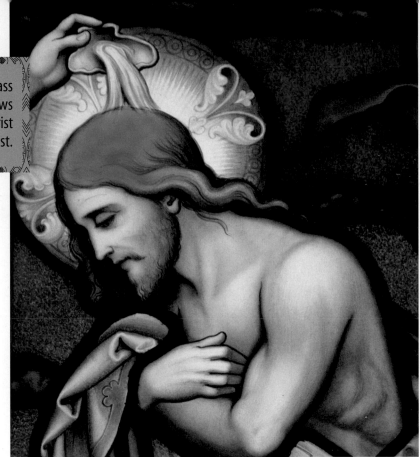

To Christians, baptism is also necessary for salvation, and to take away original sin. Jesus himself said that, 'He who believes and is baptized will be saved; but he who does not believe will be condemned.' (Mark 16:16).

There are three main branches of Christianity – Roman Catholic, Protestant and Eastern Orthodox – and within each of these branches there are many different denominations. All Christians must be baptized, but not all are baptized as babies. Members of some denominations believe it is important to wait until a person is mature enough to decide for himself or herself whether or not to join the faith.

To prepare for their child's baptism, parents may attend classes that explain the ceremony and what it represents. They then choose their child's godparents, who will take part in the ceremony as well.

FOCUS ON:
Godparents

The custom of having godparents goes back to Ancient Rome, when people began converting to Christianity from pagan religions. Converts were asked by the local bishop to have a Christian sponsor, known as a patronus ('protector') to ensure that their decision to become a Christian was sincere. When Christians began baptizing babies, in the 2nd century CE, they carried over the custom of having one or more sponsors for the child. Traditionally, godparents have been responsible for the child's religious education, but today they are seen more as people who will take a continuing interest in the child as he or she grows up. They may be related to the child, but are often close and trusted friends of the parents. In the Catholic Church, godparents must be confirmed Catholics themselves.

The baptism ceremony

Baptism takes place in a church, often during a regular Sunday service. The priest or vicar conducts the ceremony at the church's font, which contains holy water. The baptism includes a christening service, at which the child is formally named.

Though there may be variations among different denominations, most Protestant baptisms are broadly similar. The baby, often dressed in a white christening gown to represent purity, is held by one of the parents, who gather with the godparents and the vicar around the font.

Water from a font is used during a baptism. Fonts are often found near the main entrance to a church, to symbolize that baptism is the way into membership of the church.

FOCUS ON:
Water in baptism

Water is an essential part of the baptism and christening ceremonies. In some denominations the baby is just sprinkled with holy water, in others the child is completely immersed in it. Both are symbolic of Christ's own baptism in the River Jordan, but there may be deeper symbolic meanings, too. Immersing a child in water can be a symbolic re-enactment of birth – the child is reborn as a Christian. Because of its cleansing and healing properties, water is part of purification rituals in many religions.

As the vicar pours water over the baby's head, he says, 'I baptize you in the name of the Father and of the Son and of the Holy Spirit'.

The vicar begins by thanking God for the new life of the baby, and then reminds the parents and godparents of their own beliefs. The godparents promise to help the child live a Christian life.

The parents then name the child, and the vicar pours a little water over the baby's head three times, once for each part of the Holy Trinity (Father, Son, and Holy Spirit). He or she follows this by anointing the baby with holy water, making the sign of the cross on the baby's forehead and saying, 'I sign you with the sign of Christ.'

The baby's parents are now given a candle to hold, to confirm their belief in God and their commitment as Christians. The flame symbolizes the light of Christianity, and with this baptism and christening the baby has moved from the darkness into the light.

The Roman Catholic service is similar, but the baby is anointed with holy oil rather than holy water. The service also includes a prayer to cast out the power of Satan and cleanse the child of original sin.

Sacred text

We bring this child, whom God has entrusted to us, and claim for him/her all that Christ has won for us. Christ loves him/her and is ready to receive him/her, to embrace him/her with the arms of his mercy and to give him/her the blessing of eternal life.

From the Methodist service of baptism

Forms of baptism

Eastern Orthodox denominations, which include Greek Orthodox and Russian Orthodox, have a similar baptism ceremony to the Catholic service. However, there are a few differences between the two denominations.

Rather than just being sprinkled with holy water, in the Eastern Orthodox Church the baby is baptized naked and is completely immersed in the water in the font three times. Babies are baptized naked in Eastern Orthodox churches to symbolize that they were born naked from their mother's womb, and that all people are born naked from the 'womb' of God. They are immersed in the water three times to represent the Holy Trinity (Father, Son and Holy Spirit), and also recall the three days Jesus spent in the tomb before being resurrected, as a reminder that baptism is like being resurrected.

FOCUS ON:
Chrismation

Immediately after baptism in the Eastern Orthodox Church, a sacrament called *Chrismation* is performed. The baby is anointed with a holy oil called Chrism. The Chrism, which represents the Holy Spirit, is used to anoint the baby's forehead, eyes, nostrils, mouth and ears, as well as the chest, hands and feet. As he touches each point, the priest makes the sign of the cross and says, 'The seal of the gift of the Holy Spirit.'

At the end of the baptism, the baby emerges from the font reborn into Christianity. They are then dressed in new, white clothes to symbolize their new purity and life as a Christian.

In some Protestant denominations – for example the Baptist Church and some Pentecostal Churches – babies are not baptized, because it is felt that a person should be old enough to make his or her own decision about whether to follow Christ. In these Churches, babies are welcomed with a blessing and a ceremony of thanksgiving.

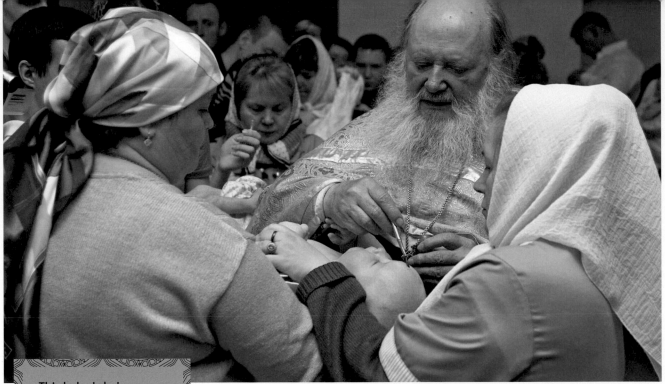

This baby is being annointed with Chrism. The oil used is specially blessed by the Patriarch (the religious head of the Eastern Orthodox Church) or by a bishop.

The ceremony of blessing and thanksgiving for a Protestant baby often takes place in church as part of a regular Sunday service. Children may also be named at their welcoming ceremony – but holy water is not used. The service includes hymns and prayers, including The Lord's Prayer, the most universal Christian prayer. Baptisms and baby blessing ceremonies are usually followed by a party or festive meal.

Sacred text

Our Father in heaven,
hallowed be your name.
Your Kingdom come,
your will be done,
on earth as in heaven.
Give us today our daily bread.
Forgive us our sins,
as we forgive those who sin against us.
Lead us not into temptation,
but deliver us from evil.
For the kingdom, the power
   and the glory are yours.
Now and for ever.
Amen.

The Lord's Prayer

Welcoming a baby boy

*I*n the Bible, God commanded Adam and Eve to 'be fruitful and multiply' (Genesis 1:28). Jews therefore see it as a duty to have children, in order to fulfil God's commandment and to make sure the Jewish people continue.

The Torah is also sometimes called the Five Books of Moses. It states that all Jewish baby boys must be circumcised.

Baby boys are welcomed into the Jewish community with a ceremony known as *brit milah*, which means 'covenant of circumcision'. Circumcision is performed when the baby boy is eight days old (unless he is ill or premature, in which case it is delayed). Circumcision is a delicate surgical procedure that involves removing the foreskin of the boy's penis. The brit milah is a reminder of God's promises to keep the Jewish people special, and a visible sign that the boy is a member of the Jewish people.

FOCUS ON:
Brit milah

Brit milah, or male circumcision, is a mitzvah or commandment, found in the Torah, the Jewish holy book. It dates back to Abraham, the first Jew, who was told by God, 'This is my covenant, which you shall keep, between me and your children after you; Every male child among you shall be circumcised… And he who is eight days old shall be circumcised among you, every male child in your generations.' (Genesis 17:10–12)

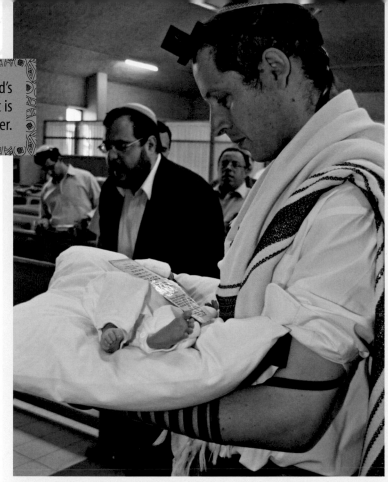

In the past, when new mothers spent more time in hospital after giving birth, the brit milah was often carried out in hospital. Today, however, the ceremony is usually held at home. It is performed by a trained person known as a *mohel*, who may be a rabbi. Today many mohels are qualified doctors.

Besides the baby's parents, the participants in the ceremony include an honoured male relative who will be the *sandek* (Greek for 'godfather'), the person who holds the baby during the ceremony. There may also be another godfather and a godmother, known as the *kvatter* (from the German gevatter, meaning 'godfather') and *kvatterin*, who bring the baby into the room. Traditionally the kvatter and kvatterin are a married couple who have no children of their own yet.

There may be an empty chair in the room, designated as 'Elijah's chair.' The prophet Elijah is said to be present at every brit milah to protect the child.

MODERN DEBATE:
CIRCUMCISION

Because circumcision is a surgical procedure performed on a very young baby, some modern liberal Jews feel it is unsafe and unnecessarily risky. They feel it should be modified or abandoned in favour of a ritual that is more symbolic.

Those in favour of circumcision argue that it is a commandment, not a choice, and one of the most ancient and revered practices of the Jewish people. Not to do it would be to go against thousands of years of tradition. They maintain that, done by a capable and experienced mohel, it is safe and hygienic.

Do you think circumcision is right or wrong?

The brit milah ceremony

*A*s the ceremony begins, the kvatter and kvatterin hand the baby to the sandek, who holds the baby on a cushion on his lap and keeps him still while the mohel performs the circumcision. The circumcision symbolically makes the baby religiously clean. After the mohel is finished, the father recites a blessing for his son.

A blessing is now said over a cup of wine, as it is at all Jewish festive occasions. The father drinks from the cup, then a few drops of wine are put on the baby's lips so that he too can take part in the blessing.

The baby is now named. Jewish children usually have two names, one in the local language of the country where they live and the other a Hebrew name, which is used on ceremonial occasions and in the synagogue when he or she is called to the Torah. The Hebrew name includes the Hebrew name of the child's father (or, for Liberal Jews, both father and mother). This emphasizes the link between the generations, an important concept for the Jewish people.

When the baby's father recites a blessing for his son, everyone else present responds with a prayer. To those of Jewish faith, it is very important that a son receives his father's blessings – an act that dates back to the time of Abraham.

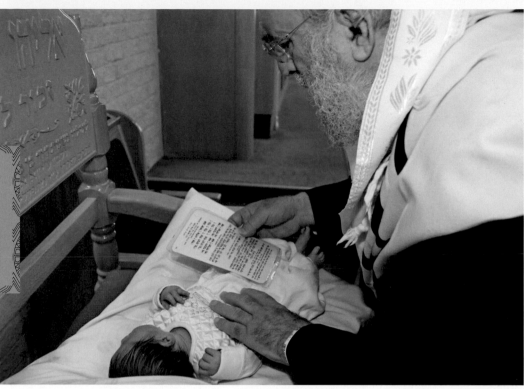

The mohel reads a prayer over the baby. The mohel will circumcise the baby, welcoming him to the Jewish faith.

Jews traditionally name their children after an honoured relative. Ashkenazi Jews (who trace their ancestry to Germany or eastern Europe) name children after relatives who have died; Sephardi Jews (whose roots are in Spain, North Africa, or Asia) may name children after living relatives.

The ceremony is followed by refreshments or a festive meal known as a *seudat mitzvah* – a meal that follows the carrying out of a commandment.

Sacred text

The father's blessing
Blessed are you, Lord our God, Ruler of the Universe, who sanctified us with your commandments and commanded us to enter my son into the covenant of Abraham.

The response:
As he has been entered into the covenant, may he come to study the Torah, enter into a marriage worthy of thy blessing, and live a life of good deeds.

15

Blessings for a daughter

In Judaism, there is no physical ritual for initiating a baby girl into the community, as there is for boys. There is a traditional welcoming ceremony, however, which takes place in the synagogue during a regular Saturday morning Sabbath service.

The baby's father is called to the Torah, along with the mother and baby. The rabbi recites a blessing for the mother and child, and the baby girl is given her Hebrew and English names. After every Sabbath service there is a *kiddush* – a ceremony at which a blessing is said over wine and a special festive bread called *challah*. When the service includes a baby naming, the baby's parents may contribute cakes, pastries and other refreshments to make the kiddush a more festive occasion.

Nowadays Jewish parents want to greet the birth of a daughter with as much celebration as there is for a boy, so some Jewish communities have introduced a more elaborate ceremony, called *simchat bat* (literally, 'joy for a daughter'). The simchat bat (sometimes called *brit bat*, 'covenant for a daughter' or *shalom bat*, 'peace for a daughter') is usually held at home and begins with the baby girl being carried into the room by an honoured female relative, often a grandmother. She is greeted with the words, '*Barucha haba*' ('Blessed is she who enters'). The baby is then handed to a close female relative who holds her throughout the ceremony.

FOCUS ON:
Shisha

Many Jews of Iraqi descent, who are mainly *Sephardi* Jews, hold a celebration for both boys and girls called *shisha* ('six' in Hebrew), on the sixth night after birth. The child is welcomed with wine and blessings. Girls are named at the shisha, and one of her parents may give a speech to explain how they chose their daughter's name. Boys are named at their brit milah two days later.

The parents recite prayers and blessings, including a prayer of thanksgiving by the mother for bringing her and her child safely through the ordeal of childbirth. The baby is given her name, after which those present respond as they do during a brit milah, with a blessing for a life of good deeds lived according to the Torah and a good marriage. The rabbi then blesses the baby. There is a blessing over wine, followed by refreshments and perhaps a seudat mitzvah.

Some Liberal and Reform Jewish families carry out a version of this ceremony in the synagogue when a boy is born as well, either in addition to or instead of the brit milah. The ceremony is held before the open Ark where the Torah scrolls are kept, to mark the child's initiation into the Jewish community and its heritage.

Sacred text

The Lord bless you and keep you;
The Lord make his face shine
    upon you and be gracious to you;
The Lord turn his face toward
    you and give you peace.

The Rabbi's Blessing, Numbers 6:24-26

First words and tastes

For Muslims, one of the main purposes of marriage is to have children. The birth of a child is seen as one of the greatest blessings of God, whom Muslims call Allah, and every child is welcomed into the family and community with joy.

There are Muslim communities all over the world, with differences in practices and traditions. But every devout Muslim, no matter where he or she lives, has a duty to pray five times a day. Prayer, or *salat*, is one of the Five Pillars of Islam – duties that every follower of the religion is obliged to fulfil. Prayer is so important to Muslims that they believe the first words every child should hear are those of the *Adhan* ('announcement' in Arabic), the call from the mosque that summons Muslims to prayer. Some Muslims believe that these were the words of the prophet Muhammad (pbuh) himself.

The sacred words whispered by a father to his baby son are said in Arabic, which is the language of the Qur'an, the Muslim holy book.

These sacred words are whispered into the baby's ears by his or her father soon after birth. They welcome the baby into the *Ummah*, or worldwide community of Muslims. Through them, the baby will understand his or her most important duty as a Muslim from the very beginning of his or her life. When this ceremony is performed by the baby's father, it also serves as an important reminder to him that he is responsible for teaching his child about the duties of their faith.

Another ceremony held soon after birth is called the *tahnik*. Something sweet – traditionally a crushed date, but a tiny piece of sugar or a drop of honey can also be used – is rubbed inside the baby's mouth, usually by a respected family member whose qualities the parents hope the baby will take on. Some families wait until the baby is brought home before performing the tahnik ceremony. However, it should ideally be performed before the baby's first feed, so in hospitals in Muslim countries, or in Western hospitals where the staff are familiar with Muslim customs, it may be held very soon after the baby's birth. Prayers and blessings follow. Tahnik is said to have been performed by Muhammad (pbuh) himself for the children of his followers. It ensures that the baby begins life with sweetness, and expresses the hope that he or she will speak sweet and respectful words.

Sacred text

Allah is most great.
I testify that there is
 no god but Allah.
I testify that Muhammad
 is the prophet of Allah.
Come to prayer.
Come to salvation.
Allah is most great.
There is no god but Allah.

The Adhan

Symbolic cleansing

At seven days old, a Muslim baby's head is shaved. This is to remove the impurities of birth, which are believed to be held in the hair, and to encourage healthy growth when the hair grows back. The shaved-off hair is weighed and traditionally the equivalent weight of silver is given to the poor. Nowadays, most families make a donation to charity, regardless of the weight of the hair.

The seventh day is also when Muslim babies are named. Names are particularly important to Muslims, because the Qur'an, the Muslim holy book, says that 'you will be called by your name on the day of judgement.' No matter where they live or what their language, most Muslims give their children Arabic names. Many of these are taken from the Qur'an, or given in honour of respected figures from Muslim history.

Muslims shave their baby's head to show that the child is a servant of Allah.

FOCUS ON:
Aqiqah

In some Muslim communities, not only is the baby's head shaved, but a ritual called *aqiqah* is performed: an animal is slaughtered as an offering to Allah. In Western countries, the meat is usually ordered from a butcher. The animal is usually a sheep; two are slaughtered for a boy and one for a girl. Some of the meat is distributed to the poor as *sadaqah*, or *zakat* – charity, which all Muslims are obliged to give. The rest of the meat is given to relatives, with some kept for the baby's close family to eat at a feast celebrating the baby's birth.

In some communities, Muslim boys are not circumcised until much later, either at the age of seven, or when they have read the entire Qur'an, which may be between the ages of ten and twelve.

FOCUS ON:
Muslim names

Muslim names tend to fall into one of four categories: names that show obedience to Allah, such as Abdullah ('servant of Allah'); names of the prophets or messengers of Allah, such as Ibrahim (after Abraham, forefather of the Muslim people; Muhammad (pbuh) gave this name to his own son); names of pious people, such as Fatimah (after Muhammad's (pbuh) youngest daughter); and names associated with desirable qualities, such as Amal ('hope') and Hariz ('strong'). Popular names for girls include Ayesha (after Muhammad's [pbuh] wife), Jamila ('beautiful'), Maimun ('lucky'), and Salima ('happy' or 'peaceful'). Popular boys' names include Anwar ('devoted to God'); Aziz ('mighty' or 'dearly loved'); Kamal ('perfection, excellence') and Yusuf ('chosen by God').

As well as being named, many Muslim baby boys are circumcised at seven days old. Muslim circumcision has the same historic roots as Jewish circumcision, as Muslims also trace their ancestry to Abraham (pbuh), through Ishmael (pbuh), his son with Hagar.

Muslim children are taught to recite short phrases from the Qur'an almost as soon as they begin to speak. They move on to learning short passages as they get older. Some boys therefore have not only read the entire Qur'an by the time they are ten or twelve, but can recite long sections of it from memory as well.

Rituals in different countries

Many Muslims have their roots in countries in Asia, North Africa and the Middle East, and all these areas have their own local customs surrounding birth and welcoming new babies. In Turkey, for example, when a child is named, a ceremony is performed by an *imam* (religious leader) or a respected elder of the family, who holds the child in the direction of Makkah (the Muslim holy city, also known as Mecca). Verses from the Qur'an are read into the baby's left ear, and his or her name is repeated three times into the right ear.

In Iran, mother and baby have a ritual bath together on the morning of the baby's seventh day. This, like head shaving, helps to remove the impurities associated with birth. If the baby is a boy, his circumcision may be performed after the bath. If the baby is a girl, her ears are pierced and gold earrings are put in. Following the earring ceremony, there is a *valimeh*, or celebration lunch, at which the main dish is made from the sheep slaughtered in the aquiqah ceremony earlier that day.

This Muslim baby is wearing clothes made from his grandfather's shirts. It is believed that the clothes will protect the baby and ward off the evil eye (see box).

FOCUS ON:
The evil eye

Many people who live in Muslim countries believe that babies are in danger of being harmed by the evil eye. This can be either an actual malicious stare, or a wish for harm made by an envious person. When the Bedouin tribespeople of the Negev desert in Israel have a baby boy, they protect him from the evil eye by hanging blue beads, meant to resemble eyes, on his head while saying prayers from the Qur'an. The *kushash* (which means 'to kick out the evil eye') are shaped like eyes, and the end of the thread that ties them is meant to resemble the baby's legs, which have the power to kick the evil eye away.

Grandfathers are especially respected among Muslims in Pakistan, and they are given the honour of choosing the baby's name. The baby's first clothes are made from one of its grandfather's shirts, in the hope that some of the grandfather's good qualities will be passed on to the child.

Muslims from Pakistan may also protect babies from the evil eye by drawing a small dot on the baby's forehead with a black powder called *kajal*.
This, it is thought, will make the baby look unattractive, so he or she will be ignored by the evil eye.

Muslims from India often tie an amulet called a *taweez* around the baby's wrist. This is a piece of black string with a small pouch attached containing verses from the Qur'an. The taweez is said to protect the child from illness.

A Bedouin family with their baby son. Baby boys are believed to be more vulnerable to the evil eye than baby girls.

Blessing a baby

Hindus believe that every human being has a soul that is reborn many times, and that each birth is a step towards joining with Brahman, the supreme spirit of the universe. Each life is marked by 16 important stages, called *samskars*. The first samskar is when a child is conceived.

The second and third samskars occur during pregnancy, and are marked in various ways. Between the third and eighth months, blessings are said to protect the new life from harm. Around the time the baby begins to move in the womb, a priest performs a ceremony during which the husband parts his wife's hair and applies a red powder called *sindur*. Holy verses called *mantras* are chanted, and music may be played to help the mother feel relaxed and cheerful. The mother is also fed nourishing foods made with clarified butter, called *ghee*, to ensure that her baby will be healthy and strong.

Some Hindu women wear red or green glass bracelets during pregnancy, because these colours are said to be lucky for the unborn baby.

The fourth samskar occurs at birth, and a ceremony called *jatakarma* is held to welcome the baby. Soon after birth the baby is bathed, then the father writes the word '*aum*' on its tongue with a golden pen dipped in honey, while he chants a blessing into the child's ear. 'Aum' is a sacred syllable that is repeated often during Hindu prayers. Mantras may also be chanted during the ceremony.

Sometimes the jatakarma ceremony is done by touching a gold spoon or ring to the child's lips, rather than a gold pen on the tongue. Whatever is used, the baby's first taste of its new world will be a sweet one.

Some time during the baby's first few days, the parents tell their priest the exact time of the baby's birth so that he can cast a horoscope (chart showing the positions of the Sun, planets and stars at birth). This horoscope will be used throughout the child's life – the first time in just a few days, when it will help with choosing the child's name. Later, it will be consulted to decide on the most favourable times for important events such as marriage, and even to help in choosing a marriage partner.

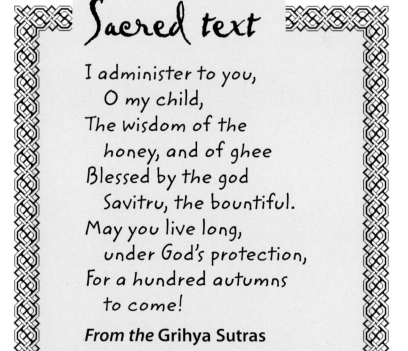

Sacred text

I administer to you,
O my child,
The wisdom of the
honey, and of ghee
Blessed by the god
Savitru, the bountiful.
May you live long,
under God's protection,
For a hundred autumns
to come!

From the Grihya Sutras

25

Choosing a name

*N*ow that the baby is a member of the family, he or she needs a name. Most Hindu babies have at least two names, and some may have as many as four.

The first name, the *nakshatra* (or 'lunar house') name, is chosen with the help of the horoscope and depends on the constellation the child was born under. The name might be that of the constellation itself, or begin with the same letter.

Each month of the Hindu calendar is devoted to a particular *deity* (god or goddess), and the baby's second name may be that of the deity for his or her birth month. The third name may be that of the family's own deity, who will protect the child throughout life.

Finally, the fourth name is the one the child will be known by to the world. It is chosen on the basis of its sound, which should be beautiful to the ear, and its meaning, which should emphasize qualities such as strength or wisdom that the parents desire for their child, or it may be the name of a deity. Often the name is chosen or suggested by the family's priest and then announced by a respected female relative.

A Hindu priest consults a horoscope chart to choose a child's name. Many Hindus believe that a name chosen by consulting the horoscope will help a child achieve his or her full potential in life.

A mother holds her baby at the namakarna naming ceremony. She will hand it to her mother-in-law to hold while the priest blesses it.

The naming ceremony, called the *namakarna*, takes place at home. The whole house is cleaned to make it pure, and the baby is given a ceremonial bath. Friends and relatives are invited to share in the ceremony.

The mother covers the baby with new cloth and wets his head to symbolize purification. She then hands the baby to her husband or mother-in-law, who holds the baby while the priest says blessings for strength and a long life. The father then whispers the baby's name, first to the mother and then into the baby's ear. In this way, surrounded by a loving family and blessings, the baby first hears the name it will carry through life.

The namakarna ceremony usually takes place 10 days from the date the child was born. It can also be carried out on 101 days after birth, or on the child's first birthday.

FOCUS ON:
The sixth day

Many Hindus believe that the sixth day of a baby's life is the most significant for deciding its future. A very delicate white thread may be tied to the baby's ankle or wrist, to symbolize the thread of life that has brought the baby to this point. When the thread falls off, it is a sign that the baby's soul has accepted this present life. A pen and a blank sheet of paper may be placed in the baby's cot on its sixth day, so that Saraswati, the goddess of knowledge, speech and the arts, can map out the child's future.

First experiences

A baby's first years are filled with many new experiences – and for a Hindu baby, some of those experiences are marked with special ceremonies.

The first time the baby is taken out – usually at around six weeks – the *nishkarmana* ceremony is held to celebrate its first glimpse of the Sun. Because the Sun is the source of brightness and sustains life, the ceremony is combined with prayers for brightness in the child's life. The outing is combined with a visit to the temple, where the priest blesses the child.

At around six months, most babies begin teething and have their first taste of solid food. In Hindu families, these events are cause for great celebration and for another ceremony, the *annaprassana*. A sweet pudding called *kheer*, made from rice boiled with milk and sugar, is put in the mouth of the child, to give him or her strength, nourishment and a taste of sweetness. This may be done as part of a festive meal for friends and relatives.

Sacred text

Salutation to you, O divine Sun, who has hundreds of rays and who dispels darkness. May you bring brightness to the life of this child.

Nishkarmana Samskar blessing, the Vedas

A baby's first haircut is another exciting experience, and another occasion for celebration in Hindu families. The *chudakarma*, or hair-cutting ceremony, takes place when the child is either one or three years old. In some families it is done only for boys. The head is completely shaved and new hair that grows is thought to give the child strength. When a baby's head is first shaved, the ceremony is celebrated with gifts for the baby and a feast for the family.

Traditionally, the baby's father does the first few snips, then the barber completes the process. The shaved-off hair may be burned as an offering to the gods.

Either in the baby's first year, or at the age of three or five, the *karnavedha*, or ear-piercing ceremony, is held, to mark the eighth samskar. This may take place in the temple or at home. Some Hindus believe that piercing the ears brings health benefits; others do it purely for decoration. In some communities, both boys and girls have their ears pierced, but in others it is done only for girls.

The child is bathed and dressed in new clothes for the ceremony, and friends and relatives are invited. The child's right earlobe is pierced first, for health; then the left earlobe, for wealth. As it is being done, the father chants a mantra, saying, 'O God, may we hear bliss with our ears'.

A baby's hair is shaved off during his or her first haircut, to physically and symbolically remove all impurities of birth and past lives.

First lessons

To a Sikh family, the birth of a child is seen as a divine gift. As soon as a Sikh mother learns that she is pregnant, she says prayers of thanksgiving and asks God to bless the child she is carrying. The child's birth is greeted with joy and blessings.

The moments after birth are some of the most important of the baby's life. In those moments, a member of the baby's family whispers a prayer called the *Mool Mantar*, which means 'basic teaching', into the baby's ear. These are the first words of the Guru Granth Sahib, the Sikh holy book, and the first words spoken during Sikh morning prayers. The prayer was composed by Guru Nanak, the founder of the Sikh religion. It is the most important Sikh prayer, so parents believe their baby should hear it before anything else.

A grandmother reads the Mool Mantar prayer to her newborn grandchild.

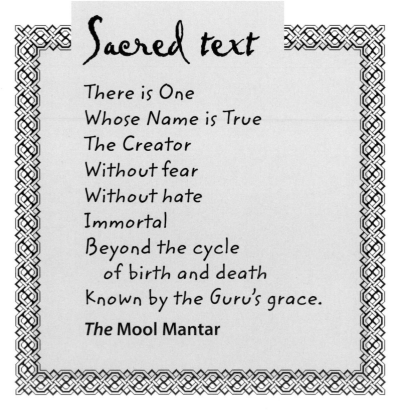

Sacred text

There is One
Whose Name is True
The Creator
Without fear
Without hate
Immortal
Beyond the cycle
    of birth and death
Known by the Guru's grace.

The Mool Mantar

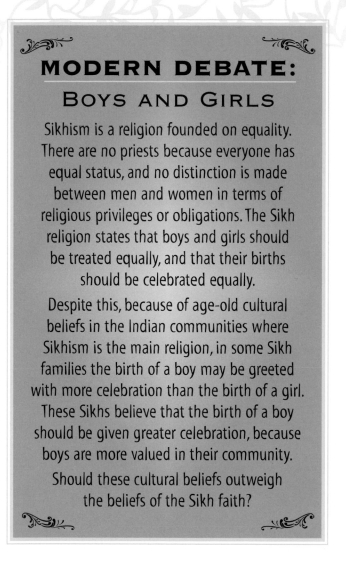

MODERN DEBATE:
BOYS AND GIRLS

Sikhism is a religion founded on equality. There are no priests because everyone has equal status, and no distinction is made between men and women in terms of religious privileges or obligations. The Sikh religion states that boys and girls should be treated equally, and that their births should be celebrated equally.

Despite this, because of age-old cultural beliefs in the Indian communities where Sikhism is the main religion, in some Sikh families the birth of a boy may be greeted with more celebration than the birth of a girl. These Sikhs believe that the birth of a boy should be given greater celebration, because boys are more valued in their community.

Should these cultural beliefs outweigh the beliefs of the Sikh faith?

Sikh girls are given equal status to Sikh boys within the Guru Granth Sahib, which states that women have the same soul as men and an equal right to spiritual education and growth.

Once the baby has heard the Mool Mantar, a family member or someone close and respected puts a few drops of honeyed water in the baby's mouth, to give him or her a sweet start in life.

The parents announce the birth of a new baby to friends and neighbours with gifts of sweets to show their joy. Relatives visit soon after the birth, bringing gifts for the baby. If it is the couple's first child, especially if it is a boy, the baby's grandparents may bring a parcel of gifts called shushak, consisting of new clothes for everyone in the family, gold jewellery for the baby and mother, and special gifts for the baby: silver cutlery and a cup, bowl and spoon.

Naming a baby

*S*ometime before the baby is six weeks old, he or she is taken to the gurdwara, the Sikh temple, to be named. As a mark of gratitude for the birth of their child, the parents bring a gift for the gurdwara. Often it is a *rumala*, a silk cloth that is used to cover the Guru Granth Sahib.

FOCUS ON:
Sikh names

All Sikh babies are given two names. Boys are given a first name followed by the name Singh, which means 'lion', and girls' names are followed by Kaur, which means 'princess'.

Many first names include words ending in '-preet' (love),'-deep' (light), and '-jit' (victory). Any name can be given to either boys or girls; only the Singh or Kaur indicates the sex of the child. This emphasizes the Sikh belief in the equality of all people – all Sikh women are the daughters of kings, and all Sikh men have the strength and courage of lions.

The naming ceremony, called *nam karan*, usually takes place at the end of a normal worship service. Hymns are sung to give thanks and to bless the new baby, and a prayer is said expressing the hope that the child will grow up to be a true and devoted Sikh. Then *amrit*, sweetened holy water, is given to the mother and baby.

A Sikh baby is given amrit during his naming ceremony. The word amrit means 'holy water' or 'water of life'.

Each Sikh child's name is found by the granthi reading the Guru Granth Sahib. When the parents and granthi choose the child's name and announce it, the congregation cheer 'Sat sri akal', meaning 'God is Truth'.

The person conducting the ceremony, known as the *granthi* because he or she reads from the Guru Granth Sahib, can be any respected member of the community. The granthi opens the Guru Granth Sahib at random and looks at the first new verse on the left-hand page. The first letter of the verse becomes the first letter of the child's name. Once the granthi and the parents have decided on the name together, it is announced to the congregation. The granthi says the words 'Jo bole so nihal' a traditional Sikh statement that can be loosely translated as, 'Whoever utters the next phrase is blessed.'

The service finishes with more blessings and hymns of thanksgiving. A popular hymn sung at baby naming ceremonies was written by the mother of Guru Arjan Dev, the Fifth Guru, when he was born in the late 16th century.

Sacred text

Dear son, this is your
    mother's blessing.
May God never be out
    of your mind, not even
    for a moment.
Meditation on God should
    be your constant concern ...
May God, the Guru,
    be kind to you.
May you love the
    company of God's people.
May God robe you with
    honour and may your
    food be the singing
    of God's praises.

Guru Granth Sahib, p.496

Sweet blessings

After the naming ceremony, *karah parshad* is given to everyone in the congregation. This is a sacred sweet pudding that is shared out at the end of every Sikh worship service in the gurdwara. When a baby is named, it is customary for the parents to provide the ingredients for the karah parshad, which is considered holy and so must be cooked at the gurdwara.

FOCUS ON:
The five K's

The five K's are:

Kesh: uncut hair, which symbolizes obedience to God by not interfering with nature.

Kangha: a wooden comb for the uncut hair.

Kachera: white shorts worn under clothes, to symbolize purity and modesty.

Kara: a steel bracelet worn on the right wrist – the circle symbolizes the eternal nature of God, and the steel represents strength.

Kirpan: a symbolic short sword that reminds Sikhs always to fight for the truth and defend the weak.

Sharing the karah parshad reminds Sikhs that everyone is equal, that God feeds people both spiritually and physically, and that God's blessings are sweet. Before cooking karah parshad, a person must bathe and put on fresh, clean clothes. After it is cooked, the pudding is marked with a ceremonial dagger, covered with a white cloth, and sprinkled with water for purity.

After the service, the parents share lunch with everyone in the *langar*, the communal kitchen and dining hall that is a part of every gurdwara. The langar is open to all, and food is free for everyone. To show that no one is higher than anyone else, everyone sits on the floor during the meal.

After the nam karan, the baby may be given a bangle. This is one of the 'five K's' that every Sikh must wear to remind them of the principles of their faith.

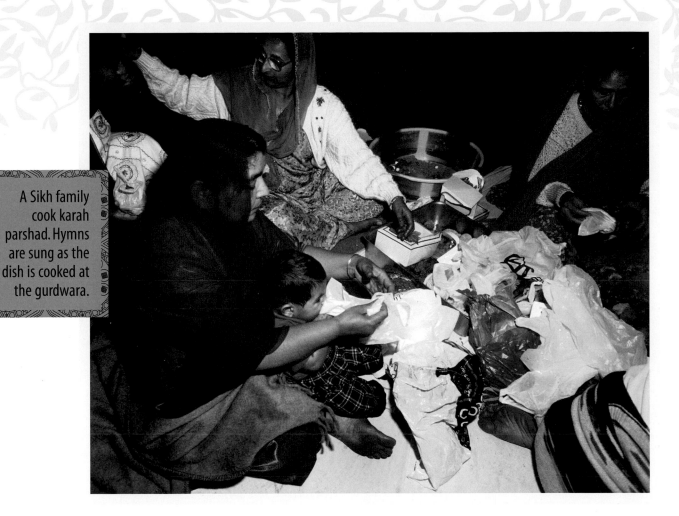

A Sikh family cook karah parshad. Hymns are sung as the dish is cooked at the gurdwara.

A very special occasion for a Sikh family with a new baby is the baby's first *Lohri*. Lohri is a northern Indian harvest festival that is celebrated in January by many Sikh families. It is a time when all Sikhs give thanks and celebrate God's bounty, and when there is a new baby in the family there is extra rejoicing. Family and friends are invited to a festive meal and party, where traditional Lohri foods such as popcorn, peanuts and sweets made with seeds and nuts are served. The parents of the baby's mother and father exchange gifts, and everyone brings gifts for the baby and the new mother. It is one more way of celebrating and thanking God for the blessing of a new life in the family.

FOCUS ON:
Karah parshad

The sweet pudding is made of equal parts of wheat flour, ghee (clarified butter) and sugar mixed with water. Some Sikhs believe that each ingredient has a symbolic significance: the sugar shows the sweetness of Guru Nanak; the ghee the richness of the Guru's teachings; and the many grains of flour the layers of complexity and meaning of the Guru Granth Sahib.

Rebirth and nirvana

*L*ike Hindus, Buddhists believe in a cycle of death and rebirth, which eventually leads to a perfect state called *nirvana* or *nibbana*. Each birth deserves a special welcome and is greeted with joy.

Buddhist parents want to give their baby a start in life that will help him or her along the path to nirvana. This often begins with taking the baby to the local Buddhist temple or the *sangha* (a Buddhist community that may include monks or nuns), to be blessed by a monk. Sometimes the monks visit the new baby at home and perform a blessing ceremony there. The blessing will be for a good life, lived according to the Eightfold Path.

A statue of the Buddha. The Buddha did not impose any religious laws, so there are very few ceremonies for life cycle events such as birth. Buddhist customs and rituals generally follow local customs.

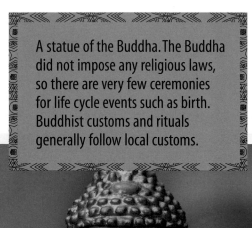

FOCUS ON:
The Buddha's birth

Siddhatta Gotama, who came to be known as the Buddha, was a Hindu prince who was born in Nepal around 500 BCE. According to one legend, Siddhatta's mother had a dream before she gave birth in which a white elephant descended from the heavens and placed a lotus flower inside the queen's body. Priests interpreted this to mean that her child would become a great emperor or holy man. Today the lotus flower is sacred to Buddhists, and the Buddha's birthday is celebrated by Buddhists throughout the world. Worshippers bring offerings of flowers to Buddhist shrines, and in some countries monks pour water over statues of the baby Buddha.

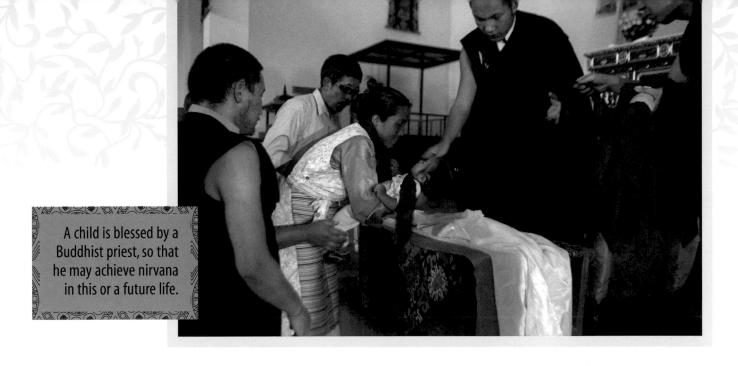

A child is blessed by a Buddhist priest, so that he may achieve nirvana in this or a future life.

In Theravada Buddhism, which is mainly practised in Sri Lanka, Cambodia, Thailand, Vietnam and Myanmar, the blessing ceremony may begin with tying an eight-strand thread (to symbolize the Eightfold Path) to a statue of the Buddha, then looping it around a water vessel. To Buddhists, water symbolizes life, purity and cleansing.

The thread is passed to all the monks present, and then to everyone else. This joins everyone together and connects them to the Buddha. Then a candle is lit, and the monks chant verses of protection and blessing for the new baby.

After the chanting, the thread is wound up and the candle is extinguished in the water. The water, which has now absorbed the light and warmth of the flame, is then sprinkled over everyone at the ceremony, and a traditional blessing known as the Verses of Victory is chanted.

Sacred text

May your future be filled with
A heaven of bright stars,
  great blessings,
Purest dawns, rewarded charity,
Unbroken mindfulness,
  clear insights...
When actions of body
  are just and true;
When actions of speech
  are just and true;
When actions of mind
  are just and true...
When all actions are just
  and true
One reaches the goal through
  justice and truth.

From the Verses of Victory

Buddhist birth customs

*O*nce the baby has been blessed, there are other customs that Theravada Buddhist families follow, particularly in Myanmar and Thailand. For example, it is traditional for the oldest members of the family, usually the grandparents, to prepare a cradle for the baby, filling it with new clothes and gifts. The gifts are chosen to symbolize the path the baby is likely to follow in life. Typical gifts for a boy are books and tools, and for a girl, needles and thread.

Buddhist parents promise to follow the teachings of the Buddha and the guidance of their ancestors in bringing up their child.

In Thailand, when the baby is a month old, another ceremony takes place in Buddhist families, either at home or in the temple. Sacred threads are gently tied around the baby's wrists and ankles as a symbol of protection for the baby's life spirit, called *khwan*.

A Japanese Buddhist temple. In Japan, where ancestors are greatly respected, some Buddhist parents take their new baby to the temple or to the graves of their ancestors.

Thai Buddhists believe that if khwan ever leaves a person's body, he or she is in great danger, so protection of the khwan must begin at the start of life.

Next the baby's head is shaved, to remove any bad influences that may have been carried over from a previous life. Thai Buddhists call this the 'fire-hair shaving' ceremony. The monk chants as the hair is being shaved off, then blesses the baby with sacred water. The hair may be wrapped in a lotus leaf and taken to a nearby river as an offering.

This is also the time for naming the baby. The monks consult the baby's horoscope to find possible names that will bring good fortune, then choose a name with the baby's parents. After the naming, parents share a meal with the monks.

FOCUS ON:
Kites in Japan

Buddhist monks brought kites to Japan in the seventh century CE and flew them to frighten away evil spirits and ensure plentiful harvests. Hundreds of years later, in the 16th century, a Japanese lord flew kites over his castle at Hamamatsu to celebrate the birth of his first son. Over time, the practice of flying kites to celebrate the birth of a first son became popular with fathers all over Japan, and this is still done today. At Hamamatsu Castle, each kite flown is dedicated to a baby boy born during the previous year.

Kite flying is part of Japanese Children's Day, a national festival held every May.

Birth and the Navajo people

Other cultures and religions around the world have their own customs associated with birth. The Native American Navajo people have lived in the southwest of what is now the United States for more than a thousand years. They still preserve many of their ancient spiritual practices and cultural traditions, including those concerning pregnancy and birth.

Sacred text

From the heart of Earth,
   by means of yellow pollen
Blessing is extended.
Blessing is extended.
On top of a pollen floor may
   I there in blessing give birth!
With long life-happiness
   surrounding me
May I in blessing give birth!
In blessing may I arise again,
   in blessing may I recover,
As one who is long life-
   happiness may I live on!

The Mother's Chant

Navajo mothers begin looking after their babies well before birth. One traditional belief is that pregnant Navajo women should not tie knots, because that will cause the umbilical cord in the womb to get tangled. Turning a weaving loom upside down would cause the baby to turn in the womb and cause a breech birth.

To prepare for birth, Navajo women have traditionally held a healing and protective ceremony called a blessingway, to keep the mother and baby safe. A version of this ceremony is still done by Navajo families today. Some non-Native American people have also begun to create ceremonies based on the blessingway.

The blessingway takes place late in the pregnancy, either shortly before the woman goes into labour or when labour has actually begun. It includes a ritual bath and singing sacred songs. Today, a Navajo woman might ask an elder of her community to perform a blessingway ceremony before she leaves for hospital. In the past, when many more women gave birth at home, a group of women including the midwife would stay with the mother while she was in labour, and the blessingway would be held then.

A red sash sprinkled with corn pollen is hung from the ceiling for the mother to hold. Corn pollen is sacred to the Navajo, because corn is the staple of their diet and an important part of their culture. The women sing songs to encourage the baby to emerge; they might also beckon to it with an eagle-feather brush. The mother chants as well. When the baby is born, the midwife gives it its first bath and anoints its head with corn pollen.

Welcoming a baby with joy has always been important to the Navajo. Soon after birth, the baby's face is gently stroked to coax a smile, so that the baby's life begins with happiness. When the baby is a bit older, the person who first makes it laugh is given the honour of preparing a special feast for the baby and the family to share.

It is traditional for Navajo babies to sleep swaddled in blankets and tied securely to a cradleboard for the first several months of their lives. In the past, this made it easy for the mother to lean the baby against a tree if she was working, or carry the baby safely on horseback.

Cradleboards are still used today. The Navajos believe a cradleboard gives the baby a feeling of security and promotes the development of a straight back.

Taoism and Yoruba babies

In China, where the religious and philosophical beliefs of Taoism began, children are cherished because they continue the family line. Taoists believe in a balance of elements in the universe, particularly the balance of yin (the feminine force) and yang (the masculine force). There are many spirits who help to keep the universe in balance, and even before birth a child is protected by a guardian spirit known as Tai Shen.

When the baby is four months old a party is held to celebrate his or her health and growth. Friends and relatives bring 'head-to-foot' presents – complete sets of clothes – and the baby's parents place offerings of peach cakes on their home altar. In Taoism, peaches are a symbol of long life. All the children at the party are given peach cakes.

The yin and yang symbol shows the balance between masculine and feminine. The black represents the dark energy of the female and the white the light energy of the male.

A big party is held on the baby's first birthday, when the baby is given its first solid food – usually a sweetened rice cake.

To the Yoruba people of West Africa, a baby is God's greatest gift. Babies are welcomed with joy and celebration at a naming ceremony that introduces the baby to the community. The ceremony, called *ko ome jade* (meaning 'bring out the child'), takes place seven days after birth for a boy, and eight days for a girl.

Names are extremely important to the Yoruba and they are chosen carefully, in consultation with community elders. All Yoruba names have a meaning that relates to something special about the baby or the family.

A Taoist shrine. A new mother may visit a Taoist shrine or temple to bring offerings to the female spirits to thank them for the safe arrival of her baby. Because the spirits are mothers themselves, it is customary to bring baby clothes for them.

FOCUS ON:
Yoruba names

Most Yoruba children have at least three names. The first is their birth name, which is chosen because of the way they were born – for example, Ige, meaning 'born in the breech position', or Ojo (male) or Aina (female), meaning 'born with the cord around the neck'. Second is the given name. This refers to a special quality of the child, or is based on family tradition or family circumstances. For example, a very big baby might be called Omoteji, which means 'big enough for two'; Yewande, which means 'mother has returned' may be given to a girl whose grandmother has died. The third name is a pet name, or 'praise name', which expresses a hope for the child. Titilayo, for example, means 'eternal happiness'; Ayoke means 'one whom everyone blesses'.

The naming ceremony is carried out with music and singing, and includes symbolic foods: kola nuts for good fortune and long life; water for purity; oil for health and strength; salt for intelligence and wisdom; honey for happiness; and liquor for wealth and prosperity. A bit of each food is touched to the baby's lips, and all the guests taste a bit themselves.

The person conducting the ceremony sprinkles water on the baby's forehead, whispers the child's name into his or her ear, then shouts it aloud for all to hear. A party follows, and friends and relatives give the baby gifts. But he or she has already been given the most precious gift – the special name that is his or hers alone.

Religion and birth: a summary

Religion	Preparation	Gifts	First experiences
Christianity	Parents may attend classes to prepare for baptism.	Gifts for baby (nappies, blankets, etc.) at baby shower. Christening gifts may include money boxes, cups, bowls and spoons.	No specific first experiences.
Judaism	No specific preparation.	No gifts are given.	No specific first experiences.
Islam	No specific preparation.	In Pakistan, baby may be given clothes made from grandfather's shirts; Bedouin boys given blue beads for protection.	Adhan whispered into baby's ear; something sweet rubbed inside baby's mouth (tahnik).
Hinduism	Blessings throughout pregnancy; father applies sindur to mother's hair parting; mantras said and music played to relax mother; mother may wear red or green glass bracelets during pregnancy for luck.	Blank paper and pen may be put in baby's cot at six days old, for goddess Saraswati to map out his or her future. Gifts given at chudakarma (hair-cutting ceremony).	Jatakarma ceremony: baby bathed, and father writes 'aum' on baby's tongue with pen dipped in honey.
Sikhism	Mother says prayers when she learns she is pregnant.	New parents give sweets to friends and neighbours; for the first baby grandparents bring shushak – new clothes for the family, jewellery for mother and baby, and cutlery, cup, bowl and spoon for baby. At naming ceremony, parents bring gift for the gurdwara, and baby given a bangle.	Mool Mantar whispered into baby's ear; honeyed water put into baby's mouth.
Buddhism	No specific preparation.	In Burma and Thailand, baby is placed in a cradle filled with new clothes and symbolic gifts, such as books, toys, needles and thread.	No specific first experiences.

Post-birth rituals	Circumcision	Choosing a name	Celebrations
Baptism and christening carried out by priest or minister in church. Includes prayers and blessings.	Circumcision not carried out in Christianity.	Name chosen by parents, given at christening.	Christening party and/or festive meal.
Brit milah ceremony for boys; simchat bat or shalom bat ceremony for girls. Includes prayers and blessings.	For boys, at eight days old.	Hebrew names often chosen to honour relatives. Boys named at brit milah, girls at simchat bat.	Seudat mitzvah (festive meal) to follow brit milah or simchat bat.
Baby's head shaved at seven days old; aqiqah – animal slaughtered and meat served at celebration feast.	For boys, either at seven days or seven years old, or when they have read Qur'an.	Usually Arabic names, often chosen from the Qur'an.	Feast that includes meat from aqiqah ceremony.
Priest casts baby's horoscope at a few days old; Namakarna ceremony at a few days old; Nishkarmana ceremony at six weeks old; Annaprassana ceremony at six months old; Chudakarma ceremony at age one or three years (for boys only); Karnavedha ceremony at age one, three or five years.	Circumcision not carried out in Hinduism.	Usually at least two names given. First letter of one of them determined by horoscope. Other name might be that of a deity, and/or chosen for its beautiful sound and meaning.	Festive meal for Annaprassana ceremony.
Nam karan (naming ceremony) held before baby is six weeks old. Includes hymns and amrit (sweetened holy water) for mother and baby. Karah parshad (sacred pudding) shared by all at the end of ceremony.	Circumcision not carried out in Sikhism.	First letter of name chosen by opening Guru Granth Sahib at random. All boys are given the second name Singh ('lion') and all girls are given the second name Kaur ('princess').	Lunch in langar. At baby's first Lohri (harvest festival), there is a festive meal and party.
Blessing ceremony by monks. In Burma and Thailand, khwan ceremony at one month old, including shaving baby's head, threads tied around baby's wrists, and blessing by monks.	Circumcision not carried out in Buddhism.	May be chosen after monks consult baby's horoscope.	No particular celebrations after birth.

Glossary

amulet charm or object thought to offer protection from illness or harm

anointing applying oil or holy water during a religious ritual or ceremony

breech birth when a baby is born feet or bottom first, rather than head first

christening Christian ceremony at which a child is baptized and given a name

covenant agreement between God and humankind in which God makes certain promises and requires certain actions in return

denominations distinctive group within one main religion

divine something that comes from God

Eastern Orthodox the national churches of Greece, Russia and some Slavic states, which grew out of a split between the two main centres of Christianity in the 11th century: Rome and Constantinople

Eightfold Path sometimes called the Noble Eightfold Path, the eight steps by which the Buddha taught that people can achieve freedom from suffering

ghee liquid part of butter that has been melted and chilled so the liquid can be separated out

Guru teacher. In Sikhism, the title is used only for the first ten Sikh leaders and the Guru Granth Sahib.

horoscope chart showing the positions of the Sun, Moon, stars and planets at a particular time. In some belief systems, the positions of these heavenly bodies are thought to influence people's lives.

imam Muslim religious leader

mantra short, sacred Hindu text or prayer chanted or recited in repetition

pagan follower of an ancient, nature-based religion

Protestant branch of Christianity that is separate from Roman Catholicism and Eastern Orthodoxy. Protestant churches do not recognize a central religious authority such as the Pope or the Patriarch, but see the Bible as the ultimate authority on Christian teaching.

rabbi Jewish teacher and spiritual leader

Reform Judaism movement to modernize Jewish practice

Liberal Judaism (sometimes called Progressive Judaism) a more modern form of Reform Judaism

rite of passage ritual or ceremony that marks a change from one stage of life to another

Roman Catholic branch of Christianity that recognizes the Pope, also known as the Bishop of Rome, as its religious authority

Sabbath Jewish religious day of rest and worship

sacrament formal religious act or ceremony that bestows a blessing on someone

Trinity in Christianity the union of three persons in one God – the Father, the Son and the Holy Spirit

umbilical cord cord that connects a baby to the mother inside the womb and carries the nutrients the baby needs in order to grow

weaning when a baby starts to eat food

Find out more

Books

Facts about Religion: The Facts about Hinduism. Alison Cooper, (Wayland, 2004)

Religious Signs and Symbols: Judaism/ Christianity/Hinduism/Islam. Cath Senker, (Wayland, 2008)

Sacred Texts: *The Guru Granth Sahib and Sikhism.* Anita Ganeri, (Evans, 2002)

The Atlas of World Religions. Anita Ganeri, (Franklin Watts, 2002)

The Lion Encyclopedia of Christianity. David Self, (Lion Hudson, 2007)

The Usborne Encyclopedia of Major World Religions. Susan Meredith and Clare Hickman, (Usborne, 2005)

World Faiths: Judaism. Trevor Barnes, (Kingfisher, 2005)

World Religions Today: Hinduism/Judaism/Islam. Gianna Quaglia, (Wayland, 2007)

World Religions Today: Buddhism/Christianity. Kathryn Walker, (Wayland, 2007)

Websites

These websites offer comprehensive information about the six major world religions, plus many other faiths. In addition, each has links to numerous individual faith websites.

www.bbc.co.uk/religion/religions

http://bible.beliefnet.com/index.html

www.religionfacts.com

This website has helpful information about rites of passage:

http://encarta.msn.com/encyclopedia_76155 7678_1____2/Rites_of_Passage.html#s2

TEACHER NOTES

- Ask pupils to find out from their parents about what happened at their own birth. Did they have a welcoming ceremony? What was it like?

- Encourage pupils to find out the meaning of their own name, and why it was chosen.

- Plan a visit to a nearby house of worship, to find out about baby welcoming ceremonies that are held there. Ask to see any special ritual objects that might be used, as well as prayer books.

- Ask pupils to list the similarities they find in birth rituals of different religions. Why do they think these similarities exist?

- Ask pupils to think about their own lives, from birth until the present. What rites of passage have they already been through? Are there any events in their life that they think should have been marked as rites of passage? How would they have marked them?

Index